IMAGES
of America

MOBILE

PHOTOGRAPHS FROM THE
WILLIAM E. WILSON COLLECTION

IMAGES
of America

MOBILE

PHOTOGRAPHS FROM THE
WILLIAM E. WILSON COLLECTION

Marilyn Culpepper

ARCADIA
PUBLISHING

Copyright © 2001 by Marilyn Culpepper
ISBN 978-1-5316-0443-1

Published by Arcadia Publishing
Charleston, South Carolina

Library of Congress Catalog Card Number: 2001087666

For all general information contact Arcadia Publishing at:
Telephone 843-853-2070
Fax 843-853-0044
E-mail sales@arcadiapublishing.com
For customer service and orders:
Toll-Free 1-888-313-2665

Visit us on the Internet at www.arcadiapublishing.com

This book is dedicated to the members past, present, and future of the Historic Mobile Preservation Society; and in loving memory of my mother, Florence Lorraine Urquhart Wheat, 1921–2001.

CONTENTS

Master photographer William E. Wilson took this *c.* 1904 self-portrait in his Mobile studio. Wilson's legacy lives on in a collection of more than 2,000 images housed in the archives of the Historic Mobile Preservation Society.

INTRODUCTION

William Ernest Wilson's camera made time stand still in Mobile at the turn of the twentieth century.

William E. Wilson was born in 1853 in London, England. His father, James Wilson, was an artist and photographer. James and his young family emigrated from England to the United States when William was two years old and they entered through the port of Charleston, South Carolina. The family settled in New York, but traveled back to South Carolina in 1861 where they lived until moving to Mobile in 1867.

The 1870 federal census lists James Wilson as a resident of Mobile. His son William is listed there as a 17-year-old photographer, following in his father's footsteps. A published advertisement in 1871 promotes J.T. Wilson's Photographic Gallery as a place where copies could be made from old pictures such as Daguerreotypes, ambrotypes, and others. He also offered services in the restoration of oil paintings, making porcelain pictures from life or other pictures, life-size paintings in pastel, framing, and painting.

As an adult, William moved to Georgia with his wife, an Englishwoman named Ellen Alice Brill. He and his family lived in Savannah where he worked as a master photographer. The family moved back to Mobile in 1894. They lived at 41 Springhill Shell Road and later on Chidester Avenue. He operated his photography business at three Mobile locations—first at 65 Dauphin Street, then 12 St. Emanuel Street, and finally at 12 South Conception Street.

In Mobile, William Wilson was a familiar figure traveling about with his camera. He reportedly shared his expertise with amateur photographers in the community and passed his photography skills on to his son, William Tristram Wilson, known as Willie, who continued to run his father's studio for a few years after William Wilson's death in October 1905.

Although much of his surviving collection is made up of unidentified portraits, Wilson's work is what we today describe as "documentary photography." This phrase was coined in the 1930s to describe the work of the Farm Security Administration. During the Great Depression such photography was used to show the American public the plight of the nation's impoverished farmers. In this respect, Wilson was ahead of his time, portraying everyday people, places, and events with clear, direct simplicity that touches the heart and elicits a sense of familiarity with the subject.

The Mobile in which Wilson plied his craft was an amalgam of change—a city in transition from a devastating war, years of post-war occupation, changing economic times, and a new era of government, commerce, and society. Wilson's photographs show Mobile during one of its most interesting periods.

Today, we marvel at the artistry of Wilson's photographs. His street scenes and architectural photographs are as striking as his portraiture. In Wilson's lens, each person evokes a dignified image, each structure seems timeless, and even the aftermath of a disaster is compelling.

As writer and historian John Sledge observed, "The marvelous images of William Wilson capture for all time the languor, grace, and quaint Victorian trappings of this now barely imaginable world. That he was here, and thought to record these scenes, is cause for celebration and delight."

Wilson's photographs are housed at the Historic Mobile Preservation Society's Minnie Mitchell Archives in the Oakleigh Historic Complex in Mobile, Alabama. Some 2,000 dry-glass negatives make up the Mobile collection of Wilson's photography from 1894 to 1905. Reproductions from the negatives have been popular among scholars, historians, and photography enthusiasts since Wilson's son gave the collection to the society in the 1950s.

Mrs. Carter Smith, archives chairman for the Historic Mobile Preservation Society in 1975, was responsible for much of the preservation of these negatives. Mrs. Smith, along with Mrs. Norman Shelton and Mrs. Richard Wells, devoted many hours to sorting, cataloging, indexing, and filing the negatives. The negatives were reproduced and stored after being assembled. The Mitchell Foundation, the archives's principal benefactor, has three times assisted preservation of the Wilson negatives through grants.

After acquisition and cataloging were complete, HMPS shared its collection with the Georgia Historical Society in Savannah and the University of Georgia Libraries Special Collections, retaining only those photographs that pertained to Mobile and its immediate region. Most of Wilson's original prints no longer exist and those remaining are damaged to various degrees. The glass negatives are fragile and some have suffered damage; therefore, his negatives have become more significant to preservationists and historians.

The creation of this book is a project intended to secure the preservation of the Wilson negative collection in Mobile. These dry-plate negatives are made of glass, commercially available in the late 1880s. In his writings about Wilson, Dennis O'Kain of the University of Georgia Department of Art describes the process as follows: "During the late 1880s the photographic printing paper commonly used was known as P.O.P. (Printing Out Process). This is a physical process, dating to the foundations of photography, based on the action of light to darken the silver sensitized photographic paper. Wilson used just such a paper: placing a negative in contact with a piece of P.O.P. paper, he would put it out in the sunlight to darken or 'print out' until the proper exposure had been reached."

With the assistance of professional photographic reproduction, HMPS made prints from the negatives in the 1970s. Prints in this book were made from these negatives. To produce this book, these prints were scanned using Adobe Photoshop on a Hewlitt Packard ScanJet 3300C scanner and a Gateway Essential computer. Reproductions of the collection are also stored by Historic Mobile Preservation Society on CD-ROM.

William E. Wilson's surviving dry-plate negatives are a unique collection of Mobile life as one century blended into the next. Reproductions of Wilson's photographs are available for a fee through the Mitchell Archives. For information, call 251-432-6161 or write HMPS, 300 Oakleigh Place, Mobile, AL 36604.

One

CITIZENS

CHILDREN

Wilson captured the c. 1900 images of Mobile's children in a charming way. In the late 1800s all was not bliss. Many families living in Wilson's time had confronted the loss of children to smallpox and other unnamed diseases. The post-Civil War period was economically strained in the city. Frequently children of working-class families held jobs to help support their families. Still, Wilson recognized that children have special qualities that transcend their circumstances. Whether his subject was the well-groomed child of an affluent family or a delightfully scruffy child, all of Wilson's children reflect a happy generation living in the midst of changing times.

This photograph of a young boy holding a book was a pose frequently used by Wilson with children. The youngster's suit is patterned after the English Little Lord Fauntleroy suit, popular in the late 1880s. It was typically made of black velvet, but wool versions were adapted in the United States. Broad-collared starched shirts and heavy black leggings completed the suit, which was considered formal dress for young boys.

Wilson's photograph of four African-American boys sitting on a fence shares the feeling of camaraderie among the children and shows the photographer's ability to authentically depict people in natural settings.

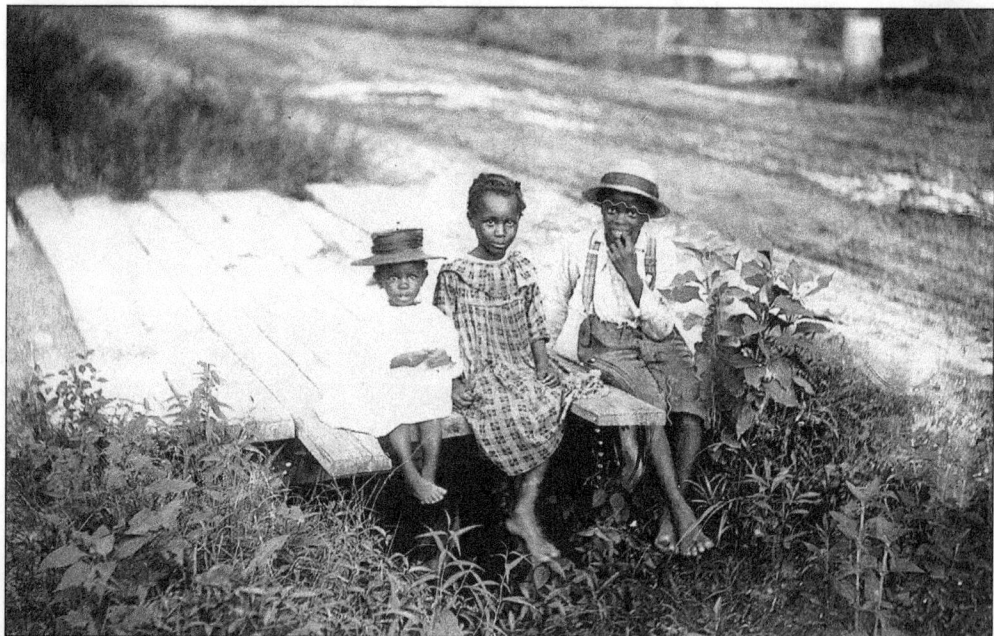

Simple wooden bridges often covered ditches and low-lying areas along Mobile's dirt roads. This photograph of three African-American children relaxing on a small bridge was typical of the lighter subjects of Wilson's wandering lens.

Photographers today could take a chapter from Wilson's stylebook with his "baby in a bathtub" photo. The picture was taken in a studio, where Wilson obviously took time to make the image stylistically and sentimentally beautiful. The unidentified baby could be boy or girl, but is obviously the apple of some parent's eye, having such a fanciful portrait taken at a tender age.

This little girl was dressed stylishly in her ruffles and lace, complete with a soft lingerie hat, and sun-shading parasol. Her short, curled ringlets were typical of those worn by children in the late Victorian period and were often accomplished with heated metal curling rods.

Wilson's camera gives equal advantage to the intricately designed porcelain dolls in lovely handmade dresses as it does to the girl who appears to take pleasure in her doll collection. The dolls and accessories were handmade and likely imported from Europe, perhaps France or Belgium.

Wilson's ability to depict his subjects at ease in informal settings is evidenced in this wonderful portrait of a young African-American lad smiling brightly with his cap tipped jauntily. An oversized coat and sagging breeches, as well as the worn boots—one of which is missing a lace—indicate economic poverty but nothing about this child indicates a lack of nurturing.

This photograph of "Mrs. Riley's nieces" shows two proper, young girls in a formal pose of the period but with softer facial expressions than often seen in similar photographs. The girls are apparently sisters and are wearing fashionable high-necked dresses and necklaces.

Wilson used unusual props in his portraits. This young girl, posed with a zither and kitten, appears natural in the surroundings, which were likely not her home but Wilson's studio. (A zither is a musical instrument composed of a flat sound box with about 30 to 40 strings stretched over it and played horizontally with the fingertips, a thin piece of metal or bone, or a bow, or set into vibration by the wind.)

Another unusual approach to portrait photography used by Wilson was having subjects pose in non-traditional ways while appearing perfectly natural with the setting. This primly dressed little girl perches pensively on the arm of a bench, certainly unlike the way her mother would have her sit at home.

Mobile Military Institute students are shown concentrating on their studies at the school on Ann Street. MMI was the forerunner of other private schools for young men and was operating in Mobile as early as the 1880s.

Wilson frequently had his subjects hold flowers, as is the case with this boy in a sailor suit. The effect resulted in a softer, yet active image. Sailor suits were popular for boys and girls from the 1860s through the Edwardian period of the early twentieth century.

LADIES

Mobile women living in Wilson's time were busy rearing children and managing households. Their lives included church and social activities. Some of them joined the work force as teachers, nurses, stenographers, and other traditionally female positions. In 1904 a chapter of the Young Women's Christian Association "in service for girls of the world" was organized in Mobile. Originally an organization for businesswomen, it soon expanded its activities to provide activities and programs for all women.

Mrs. Donnie Parker, front, and an unidentified friend posed for Wilson in his studio dressed as if they are ready to go for a ride in wintry weather. The tailor-made double-breasted suits of wool or tweed with narrow sleeves became popular in the 1880s. The wide-brimmed hats here are dressed with fabric flowers, left, and ostrich feathers.

Although it appears posed, this photograph may have been the result of one of Wilson's well-known sojourns around the city with his camera. Mrs. S. Wilson, above, is pictured on the porch of her residence at Rapier and Palmetto Streets with two house servants, a female dog, and its pups.

Lovely Miss Bussu is wearing a large-rimmed hat with a flat brim and scarved crown, secured by an enormous hatpin, which indicates the photograph was made *c.* 1904, when such a hat would have been coming into fashion.

Miss Reba Neville's portrait is a wonderful study in the newly emerging Edwardian era of fashion. Her soft, full-brimmed hat bedecked with feathers, although large, would be small compared to hats coming into fashion by 1910. The frilly high neckline, ornamented bodice, and lace-edged cuffs with more lace falling over her wrists were typical of the return to romantic dressing after the turn of the century.

Miss Zemma Mastin is shown here seated in a carriage in front of her family's home on Government Street. Miss Mastin, the daughter of a physician, never married and lived a long life in the house.

African-American women living in Mobile at the turn of the twentieth century typically worked as domestic helpers in white households. Long before white women entered the work force, African-American women were at least contributors, if not the sole support, of their families. Here, an African-American woman is shown in an attractive print dress with a beautifully dressed young child. The two may be on their way to Sunday worship services.

This elderly African-American woman may be carrying a sack of vegetables or laundry. Frequently domestic workers carried their employer's laundry to their own homes to wash and returned it the following day.

Whether this is a wedding portrait or simply a studio photograph is unknown, but the young African-American woman depicted is striking. The slight-V neckline with stiff lace and over-the-elbow length of her sleeves indicate the picture was taken about 1898 or later.

Wilson's subject is dressed for a special occasion, perhaps for "Sunday-go-to-meeting," or a formal family gathering. The lace collar and leg-o-mutton sleeves were fashionable earlier than the c. 1900 photograph was made but the image is nonetheless attractive. Based on lighting and background shadows, the photograph was apparently taken outdoors.

GENTLEMEN

Mobile men of Wilson's time were involved in a variety of professions as the city's economic base broadened from cotton to lumber and other forest products and manufacturing. Various workers, including bankers, commission merchants, ministers, lawyers, doctors, laborers, and barbers, as well as men at their leisure, found their way in front of Wilson's camera lens. Fraternal organizations gained popularity in Mobile in the late 1800s and many men divided their energy among family, work, and civic efforts.

Two men pause with a pair of fine oxen harnessed between them. As an emerging producer of lumber, Mobile relied on its "natural" heavy equipment—teams of oxen and mules—which had previously been relegated to more traditional agricultural pursuits such as row-crop farming and pulling wagons later for assistance in the forestry industry.

Wilson took this c. 1903 photograph of Joe Kuntz in fraternal regalia behind Kuntz's Mobile house.

This pair of gentlemen was so proud of their string of fish that they apparently dressed up for the occasion and brought the stringer, as well as their fishing poles, into the studio for a portrait commemorating the day. Whether the unidentified men shared their catch—or a cigar—with Wilson is not known.

Mayor Patrick J. Lyons, pictured in the rear left, traveling in his car with a driver and unidentified friend, was one of the most popular of Mobile's elected officials. Lyons was first elected to the city council in 1897 and became mayor in 1904. He served two terms, then returned in 1913, 1915, and 1917 when the city moved to a commission form of government. Lyons had a colorful background. The child of Irish Catholic immigrants, he went to work as a deckhand on a riverboat at 13. A hard-working, industrious youngster, he rose through the ranks to become a captain and later part owner of a riverboat line. He successfully operated the riverboat packet "Maggie Burke" until the mid-1880s. He returned to the city as a young man around the mid-1880s and took up proprietorship of a local grocery store. Quickly he became a leader in the business community and first became a member of the council through appointment in 1894. He was active in civic affairs, too, serving as vice president of City National Bank, a member of the Knights of Columbus and other organizations.

Above, left: William J. Kilduff, pictured here, was a yard clerk for Heironymus Brothers. Hieronymus brothers William, George, and Henry, were lumber dealers and proprietors of saw and planing mills in Theodore at the corner of Madison and Water Streets.

Above, right: Businessman Joseph Darling, wearing a high starched collar, bow tie, and a single-breasted wool coat without vest, is a picture of the subtle transition in men's day wear at the turn of the century.

Right: Ross Dodson, photographed by Wilson c. 1900, appears dressed for a formal evening, perhaps a Mardi Gras ball.

This distinguished young African-American man was likely a member of Mobile's relatively small population of educated blacks at the turn-of-the-century. He may have been a teacher, preacher, or businessman. His tweed jacket, starched white shirt, and neat bowtie, as well as his clean-shaven appearance, indicate he was a man of means.

This colorfully dressed African-American man known as "Bottles" was a frequent inhabitant of the city's waterfront scene around 1900.

Cudjoe Lewis, photographed outside his house by Wilson c. 1905, was a living reminder of slavery as well as the strength of character to overcome diversity. Lewis, referred to as "the last slave," was kidnapped from Africa and smuggled into Mobile on the slave ship Clotilda in 1859. Once here, he and other free blacks formed their own community near Mobile named Africa Town. Although he often professed a desire to return to his homeland, Lewis and his wife, Celia, raised a family in Africa Town, where he lived until his death in 1935.

This *c.* 1900 photograph depicts a group of African-American men who have apparently assembled for a religious meeting. Whether this was a group of clergymen or a single minister (front row, center) and his deacons or vestry members, this is an imposing group. After the Civil War, a majority of African-Americans living in Mobile chose to form their own congregations and worship independently of the white population. At the turn of the century, African-Methodist Episcopal, Baptist, and other predominantly black congregations were thriving in the city.

COUPLES

In Wilson's time, brides and grooms, not unlike couples of today, wanted to capture their special event in photographs. Wilson's collection of Mobile wedding photographs does not include the names of the couples depicted. Following are three examples of Wilson's photography commemorating wedding days for turn-of-the-century couples.

This bride wore what was sometimes referred to as a "lawn gown," with ruffled lace tiers from below the knee to the hemline. Her sleeves are three-quarter-length, indicating the wedding took place post-1900.

Two couples, posed differently, each produced beautiful portraits through Wilson's lens, c. 1900. The groom's white tie and gloves in hand at right indicate dancing likely followed the nuptials at the evening's reception.

Two

COMMUNITY

RESIDENCES

In the post–Civil War years, Mobile's population growth slowed. In 1860 the population numbered 30,000 but by century's turn had only grown to 39,000. Economic change came slowly and life had its difficulties for Mobilians, but the character of the houses constructed and inhabited in Wilson's time showed an appreciation of place that transcends economic hardship.

Perhaps the 19th century Irish poet William Allingham, in writing sentimentally of leaving home, could have as easily been referring to Mobile when he wrote, "The kindly spot, the friendly town, where everyone is known/ And not a face in all the place but partly seems my own." Wilson's Mobile was small when compared to emerging cities such as Birmingham and Atlanta, but its rich blend of ethnic groups and Gulf Coast setting created a unique and lovely culture that is reflected in its residences.

Minnie Hatch McCartney, the widow of attorney Thomas N. McCartney, owned this Queen Anne residence that once stood on Government Street east of Broad Street at Hamilton Street. Built in the late 1870s, it is no longer standing.

The wonderful Queen Anne-transitional Wefel residence seen in this c. 1902 photograph is still standing on Dauphin Street.

This residence was constructed on "new" Government Street (now Airport Boulevard), west of Ann Street, facing Memorial Park. It once belonged to George Fearn and was later sold to Edgar Flynn.

This stately house on Government Street once stood at the southwest corner of Jackson Street and was the home of Mayor Samuel Garrow in the mid-1800s. Garrow was a native Virginian and it is the Tidewater region of his home state that obviously influenced the design of this house, which was distinctive amidst houses built with the humidity of the Gulf Coast in mind. Garrow held a lavish reception at this house when the Marquis de Lafayette was entertained there in April 1825. Lafayette, a hero of both the American and French revolutions, was invited to visit the Gulf Coast city while he was touring the east coast of the U.S. He came to the city and was lavishly entertained. It has been written that Lafayette declared Mobile's ladies "the fairest in America." Later, the house was sold to the Mikle family and eventually demolished. Today its site is a commercial one.

These fine residences were located on the south side of Government Street, west of Marine Street, c. 1899. The house under construction was owned and occupied by Mr. and Mrs. Thomas McMillan. Mrs. William J. Hearin Sr. was the first of four generations to reside at the home in the center. The house to the right was the home of cotton factor J.A. Watters, but would later be converted into one of Mobile's first apartments by the Hearin family. The entire site is now part of an office building known as 951 Government Street.

In 1902, attorney Richard H. Clarke occupied this wonderful house on Government Street across from George Street. Banana baron Ashbel Hubbard had architect George Rogers remodel it in 1925 and it later served as the headquarters for the YWCA.

Located at 350 Palmetto Street, this grand house was occupied by the Henry Hybart family *c.* 1900.

Murray Forbes Smith, the father of Alva Smith Vanderbilt, purchased these ornate French oak furnishings around 1848. Smith built a distinctive Gothic Revival house on Government Street at Conception. At the top is a parlor set; below left, is a corner étagère, and below right, is a bookcase.

FAITH

In the mid-nineteenth through early twentieth century, Mobile's population was a mixture of faith groups. Predominantly Roman Catholic from its founding, Mobile in the nineteenth century saw an increase in the number of Protestants among its population, with non-Catholics becoming the majority.

Ethnically diverse Catholic congregations continued to populate numerous parishes citywide. White and black Protestants worshipped separately in churches of various denominations including Methodist, Baptist, Episcopalian, and Presbyterian. The small Jewish community in Mobile began its major growth era with the arrival of Alfred G. Moses as rabbi in 1901.

African Americans of the late nineteenth century, emerging as a free culture, largely maintained independent religious congregations from the white population of Mobile. Before slavery ended many blacks worshipped at church services conducted by whites for whites, they were required to sit apart in the church sanctuaries, usually in a balcony or area segregated from the white worshippers by a low wall. The practice of outdoor baptizing, shown here, was a common one among evangelical Protestant blacks and whites of the antebellum period and into the twentieth century, particularly among Baptists and other faiths which require full-body submersion for the baptismal rite.

The congregation of First Christian Church constructed this sanctuary at the southwest corner of Government and Dearborn Streets in 1906. The building became the Hellenic Orthodox Church in 1927 but was replaced with a parking lot in the 1960s. St. Francis Street Baptist, shown below, c. 1900, was built in 1848. This building was the denomination's third attempt at success in establishing a permanent meeting site. In fact, this building was financed by funds contributed by affluent members of other denominations.

Wilson photographed the majestic interior of Big Zion A.M.E. Zion Church, located on Bayou Street, c. 1900. It was one of the earliest traditional African-American churches in the city. The national church "A.M.E.," which stands for African-Methodist-Episcopal, was established in 1816 by Richard Allen. Allen, a former Pennsylvania slave who worked to buy his own freedom, was also the denomination's first bishop.

Broad Street Methodist Church, at the southwest corner of Broad and Elmira Streets, had the quaint, serene character of a country church at the edge of the city. It was built in 1890, the congregation having moved from St. Paul's Methodist at Canal and Jefferson Streets. Hurricane Frederic destroyed this building in September 1979.

Wilson's photograph, above, shows the Romanesque exterior of the Sacred Heart Chapel at Visitation Monastery on Spring Hill Avenue, as well as its beautiful interior below. A convent (residence for members of the Visitation Sisters, a religious order which originated in France) was founded at the monastery in 1832 and housed a school for girls.

The tabernacle in Sacred Heart Chapel sits atop an altar with steps leading up—all composed of Italian white marble. Images of prayerful angels kneel at either side.

Wilson's collection contains several views of Visitation Monastery. Perhaps this serene garden on the Visitation grounds gave rest and refreshment to the photographer and other visitors, as well as to the monastery's residents.

An impressive crowd gathered for the laying of the cornerstone for the new Jewish temple at 559 Government Street in 1902. Constructed under the leadership of Rabbi Alfred G. Moses, the new location moved the Jewish congregation's site of worship from its original Jackson Street temple, built in 1858.

Once completed, the temple provided a place of worship for Mobile's Jewish population, which has had a presence in the city since the early nineteenth century.

Government Street Presbyterian Church was constructed in 1836 by noted architects James Gallier and the brothers Charles and James Dakin. It is considered one of the finest examples of Greek Revival architecture in the South. Prominent lawyer, judge, and politician Henry Hitchcock was a major contributor to financing its construction. Hitchcock, a grandson of Ethan Allen, served as secretary of the Alabama Territory in 1816. He was largely responsible for the construction of this magnificent church, Barton Academy, and several other significant early buildings of Mobile. The church remains an active one.

The Daughters of Mercy religious community came to Mobile at the invitation of Bishop Dominick Manucy in 1884 after Mother Mary Austin Carroll, superior of the New Orleans community, established a school in Pensacola in 1877. By 1895, the Mother House (above) of the order had been established in Mobile on St. Francis Street at Bayou Street. The order moved locations in the mid-1900s and the Empress Chandelier Company later occupied the original building. It is currently being renovated for use as a luxurious multi-unit residential complex.

MAGNOLIA CEMETERY

Ceremonial burying of the dead is an ancient tradition among many faiths. Magnolia Cemetery, which dates to 1825, when it was referred to as "the new burying ground," began burials in 1836. The funerary art in Magnolia Cemetery is known around the world. Many notable Alabamians including Confederate Gen. Braxton Bragg, author Augusta Evans Wilson, and Walter and Bessie Bellingrath are buried here. The cemetery receives hundreds of visitors each year.

In Wilson's day Mobile already had a well-established public cemetery in Church Street Graveyard and the Catholic Cemetery, as well as the National Cemetery near what became Magnolia Cemetery. Still, it is the photographs of scenes in Magnolia that are the best of the collection relating to cemeteries.

The Working Man's Timber and Cotton Benevolent Association erected this handsome monument around 1901. Building committee members were Thomas H. Martin, president; William E. Davis, vice president; E.G. Dreaper, treasurer; Robert Devine, financial secretary; Calvin Norris, recording secretary; Charles Hamilton, chairman of the building committee; James Glass; and Thomas J. Rowell.

"Decoration days" are an old tradition in Southern cemeteries. These floral decorations were placed in Magnolia Cemetery c. 1900.

Confederate Rest at Magnolia Cemetery remembers those who died defending the South in the Civil War, many of them members of the earliest families of Mobile.

MEDICINE

The history of medicine in Mobile is a major portion of the history of medicine in Alabama. Many notable physicians have practiced in the Port City and the development of hospitals in the early nineteenth century established Mobile as a significant regional medical center. Among Mobile's most famous physicians are Dr. Jerome Cochran, the "Father of Public Health in Alabama," Dr. Josiah Nott, a pioneer in the fight against malaria and yellow fever, and Dr. William C. Gorgas, a leader in the eradication of smallpox.

A strong medical community, supported by investment in well-equipped hospitals devoted to patient care, research, and community outreach, has been a tradition in Mobile since before Wilson's time and remains the standard today.

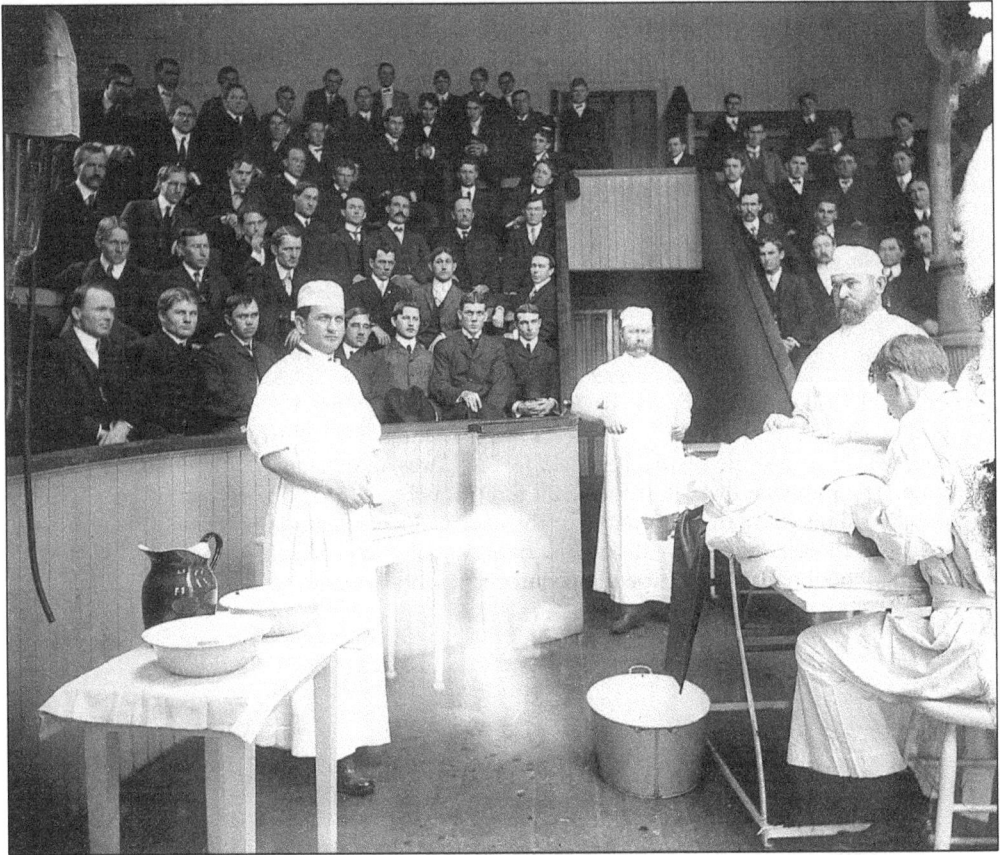

Drs. Howard, Frazer, and Jackson demonstrate a surgical procedure for medical students and photographer Wilson, c. 1902.

The Medical College of Alabama, located at 550 St. Anthony Street, was opened in 1859. Founded by Dr. Josiah Nott and colleagues, it was a branch of the University of Alabama. Nott, a co-founder of the Mobile Medical Society in 1841, was an outstanding figure in the world of medicine. The physician, who lost four children through yellow fever, devoted years of his life to its study and his research contributed to the eventual identification of mosquitoes as carriers of the deadly disease. Nott served on the college faculty and dedicated much of his time to making the school one of the best-equipped medical schools in the country.

When the old Spanish Royal Hospital was abandoned, the United States built a new hospital on St. Anthony Street. The U.S. Marine Hospital was completed in 1842. One of the oldest hospitals in the States, it later housed a tuberculosis hospital and now serves as the headquarters of the Mobile County Department of Human Resources.

Wilson photographed Dr. John A. Rush, one of Mobile's first urology specialists, in his office at the turn of the century.

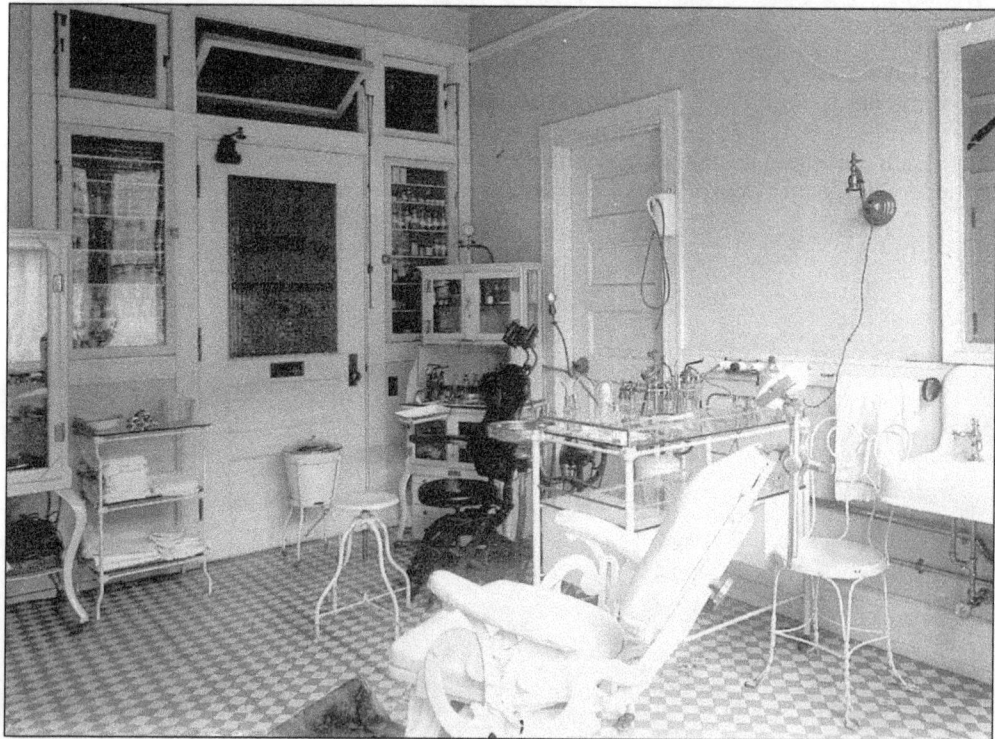

The office of Dr. T. Aubrey Dickson, a graduate of Tulane Medical School who practiced in Mobile, looks considerably different from modern medical offices.

Nurses pose in front of the new Providence Hospital constructed in 1902 on Springhill Avenue. (The original hospital was on St. Anthony Street and dated to 1854.) Providence was established after a brief tide of anti-Catholic sentiment led to the city council's action to drive the Daughter's of Charity from the management of the city hospital. Rather than dignifying the attacks—which had been motivated by a short-lived national movement called the "Know Nothing Party"—Bishop Michael Portier established Providence , which remains a strong presence in Mobile's medical community today.

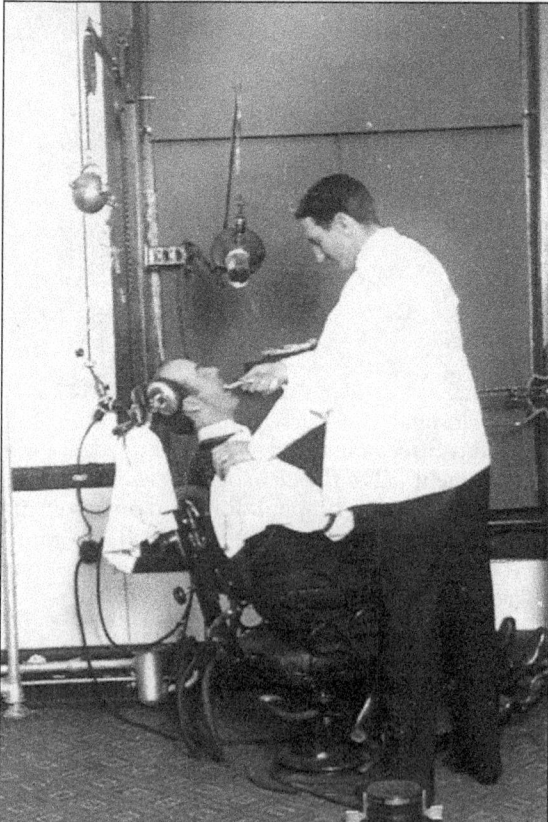

Specialists in various fields of medicine practiced in Mobile during Wilson's time. A dentist, left, examines his patient; Wilson's photograph, above, shows the interior of an ear, nose and throat doctor's office.

Three

COMMERCE

STREETS

Mobile's economy was showing marked improvement by the late nineteenth century. Electric streetcars replaced mule-drawn cars in 1893, allowing the development of prosperous suburbs west of Broad Street and beyond the city limits. Dauphin Street would remain the city's premier shopping district until the arrival of shopping malls in the early 1960s. By that time diesel buses had long replaced the charm of the electric trolleys. —Tom McGehee

Conductor and driver await passengers for a streetcar on Wilkinson Street (now Washington Avenue), c. 1894. Electric streetcar cables were installed in 1893.

This is an early view of Dauphin Street, facing east from Royal, with cable car lines and horse-and mule-drawn vehicles present.

Government Street west of Water Street offered a central refueling spot of sorts where horses, mules and even people could stop for water at a public fountain. (The monument to Admiral Raphael Semmes by Casper Burberi, unveiled in 1900, is visible in the distance.)

This photo shows Royal Street, south of Dauphin, with electric streetcars, wagons, and pedestrians. This photo includes turn-of-the-century businesses Zadek Jewelry, the Hotel Royal, Hammel's Department Store, and the furniture emporium of Adam Glass, in the former Odd Fellow's Hall.

Wilson documented the installation of sewer lines on Dauphin Street between Royal and Water Streets.

Geese cross Old Shell Road at Herndon Avenue.

Bay Shell Road in the late 1800s was a toll road. It was eventually washed away in a hurricane.

A cable car, early automobile, and attractive residences are complemented by a handsome line of trees looking east on Dauphin Street, west of Common Street.

Conception Street at the square, facing north is seen in this photograph. The stately Cawthon Hotel is visible down the street on the far left.

PUBLIC BUILDINGS

Mobile entered the twentieth century with an optimistic outlook. Fortunes were being amassed in the ever-growing import and export of lumber and bananas, and the new mansions on Government Street reflected the propserity.

The city's skyline began to change rapidly with the five-story Masonic Building in 1902, the seven-story City Bank Building in 1903, and finally the towering Van Antwerp Building at 10 stories in 1906. A hotel boom brought the Bienville in 1900, the Cawthon in 1906, and the palatial new Battle House in 1908.

Wilson's numerous photographs of shops, waterfront merchants, and the arrival of the automobile reflect the period and its excitement. Only the tragedy of a World War would overshadow it.
—Tom McGehee

The U.S. Custom House, completed in 1856, and the City Bank Building of 1903, dominate this view of Royal Street south of St. Francis Street. The debris from the Battle House fire of 1905 in the foreground dates the photograph. The First National Bank of Mobile absorbed the bank in 1915 and finally demolished the block for its tower in 1964.

The Old City Prison and Police Station with guardhouse, located on Conti Street looking west, was demolished in 1895.

This 1905 view of Commerce Street is dominated by the new warehouse of the T.G. Bush Grocery Company. The brick building to the left housed the Chamber of Commerce and Cotton Exchange and dated to 1866. Rudolph Benz was the building's architect. The roof of the building had the figure of a cotton bale with a crown on it, modeled after the Mardi Gras King's crown, to emphasize that "cotton was king" in Mobile. It also had a statue of the "Goddess of Mobile's Industry." The goddess stood on an anchor and held a wreath over her head to symbolize the city's commerce by land and sea. A fire took the Chamber of Commerce; urban removal in the 1960s took the rest.

Mobile County Courthouse was a unique structure. Described by its architect Rudolf Benz as "German Renaissance," the building was a mixture of lines and accents. Its features included marble floors, stained glass windows, and a 186-foot clock tower. Its statuary included lions that have been restored by the Friends of the Museum of Mobile for display. The building was damaged by a hurricane in 1906 and demolished to make way for new construction in 1958.

Barton Academy, Alabama's first public school was constructed in 1835–1836. A striking Greek Revival structure, it is located on Government Street and was named for Willoughby Barton, who was the author of the 1826 bill that provided for public education in Mobile.

Springhill College is one of the first two colleges in Alabama and the oldest Catholic college in the South. Bishop Michael Portier established it in 1830 as St. Joseph's College on Spring Hill. It was renamed Springhill when the Jesuits assumed control of the school in 1847. The administration building, pictured here, replaced the original, which was destroyed by fire in 1869.

BUSINESSES

Businesses were concentrated in the downtown area and along the waterfront during Wilson's time of recording Mobile's history. Mobilians could find just about anything a family would want in the city's various shops. Although the city did not have what today would be described as a "convenience store," customer service extended to home deliveries from many establishments, which certainly heightened convenience to shoppers.

Brokers, thanks to available rail service, could provide wholesale distribution from Mobile directly to cities as far away as Chicago in a matter of days. Mobile was a window to the world for commerce, thanks to its port and railroads.

Top: Wilson photographed the Gulf Mobile & Ohio Railroad terminal as it neared completion in 1905. Completed in 1907 north of downtown, it reflected a Spanish influence with ornate exterior and orange tile roof.

Bottom: Wilson's bird's eye view of the city, probably taken from the roof of the Cawthon Hotel, shows the Cathedral of the Immaculate Conception as the focal point of downtown, c. 1900. Today's Cathedral Square is a beautiful park surrounded by quaint shops, restaurants, and offices. Bishop Portier's residence, a Gulf Coast (also known as Creole) cottage built in the nineteenth century, is also located on this square.

Yocker's Grocery on Jefferson Street, above, was typical of the retail markets which thrived in Mobile in the late nineteenth century. Here, a young girl poses for Wilson at the base of a tower of various canned goods while surrounded by large watermelons. The store is virtually filled to the ceiling with offerings for customers. An ornate sculpture, left, on the exterior wall of Peerless Laundry added a whimsical touch to the city's architectural face.

E.M. Johnston & Co., right, a wholesale liquor distributor on Commerce Street, poked fun at itself with this float (above) depicting a trio of revelers endorsing its products.

Robert Berney & Company offered sturdy wagons and fine carriages like the ones on display outside its building, *c.* 1898.

Adam Glass, front and center, poses with his employees from the A. Glass House Furnishings Store. Glass was a German immigrant who opened his first store at 40 Dauphin Street, then moved into the former Odd Fellows Hall on Royal Street between Conti and Dauphin Streets. The second location was referred to as "The Cream of the World's Best Furniture Markets" in Wilson's day.

Cunningham Hardware was located on Commerce Street, which vanished with urban renewal.

Wilson captured a busy street scene in front of Joseph J. Aynsley Process Engraving Co. A newsboy and several men stop to pose for the photograph. What is being hauled in the wagon is not clear, but the fact that there are four mules hitched for the hauling indicates it is a heavy load.

The turn-of-the-century brought automobiles into the mainstream of American life and Mobilians were not to be left behind. Gunthorpe & McKean, Electrical Contractors, expanded its offerings to include automobiles.

When Southern Automobile Company arrived on South Conception Street, the horseless carriage was still a luxury.

Operators connected citizens via the Home Telephone Company switchboard.

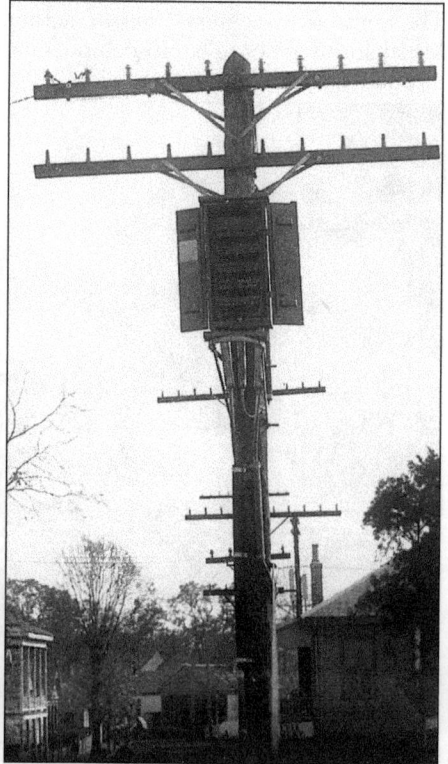

Generators, left, and telephone poles like this one, right, were signs of progress Wilson documented.

The magnificent Van Antwerp
Building—known as Mobile's
first modern skyscraper—is shown
under construction in 1905. It
was completed in 1908 and had
10 stories of reinforced concrete.
Built by Garrett Van Antwerp,
a pharmacist, the building was
covered with terra cotta tiles. It
is an example of the Chicago
or commercial style of
architecture. This building
replaced the one below.

The original Van Antwerp's
Drugs at 2 South Royal Street
offered a variety of products from
medicines to gardening supplies
for Mobile families.

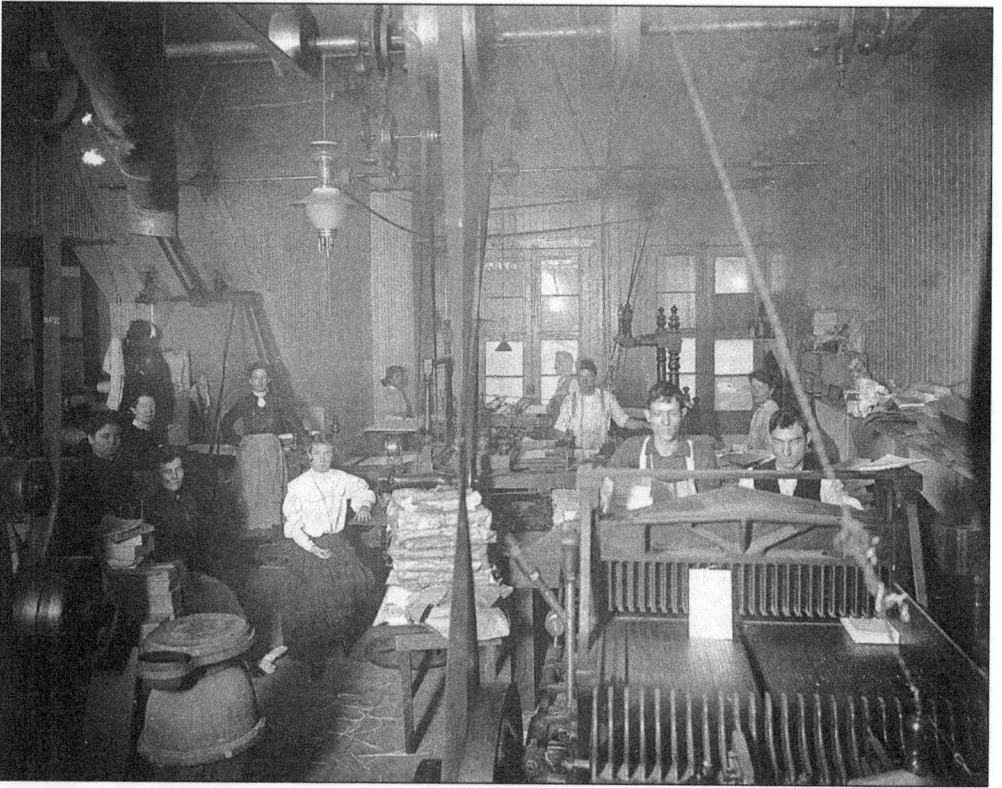
Employees of Wilbur W. Gill's print and binding shop pause from work to pose for Wilson's camera.

The *Mobile Register*, one of the city's daily newspapers in Wilson's time and the only one still in circulation today, was reliant upon its team of carriers or "newsboys" to get the paper to customers.

BELTING, PACKING, HOSE, CHAINS & DOGS.

WALTER A. ZELNICKER SUPPLY CO. OF ALA.

STEAMSHIP SUPPLIES & CORDAGE

Walter A. Zelnicker Supply Co. of Alabama, a commission merchant, offered a variety of steamship supplies and cordage. Domestic and international trade by water defined the demand for such supplies—and the sheer size of Zelnicker's operation. At the turn-of-the-century, Mobile goods were being transported up the Alabama River as well as through its seaport.

A clear sign of Mobile's international trade is evidenced in this photograph taken by Wilson c. 1902. Armour Packing Company, a meatpacking giant, shared this location at the foot of Government Street with United Fruit Company. United Fruit offered direct connection with the West Indies, Central, and South America. Rail and water were the important modes of transporting goods at the time and this location made ample use of both.

Alabama Manufacturing Company's Oak Grove sawmill and lumberyard met the growing demands for Southern lumber that became an important part of Mobile's trade base at the turn of the century.

Mobile Coal Company operated this coal yard and supplied coal to businesses in Mobile and shipped it by railcar to points outside the area.

Employees of Arnold's Shoe Store were prepared to fill customer needs with an impressive inventory that surrounds them on each wall.

Hammel's Department Store was constructed on Royal Street south of Dauphin Street in 1902. Leopold Hammel, a Bavarian-Jewish immigrant, owned it. The store was already one of the major retail businesses in Mobile for 27 years when it moved to this location. Shopping at Hammel's was elegant, with patrons seated while sales clerks presented items for consideration. Deliveries were made promptly to the customers' home by horse-drawn wagons.

This photograph of North Royal Street shows the boarding and sale stables of John L. Ramsey and the McDonald brothers. Even though automobiles had arrived in Mobile, horse- and mule-drawn wagons remained an important part of Mobile commerce and delivery, as well as conventional transportation for many families.

Employees pose for Wilson in front of the Door, Sash & Blind Factory on North Water Street owned by Freeman and John Turner.

Commission merchants, or "factors," were among the prosperous businessmen along the Gulf Coast in the late nineteenth century. They acted as agents for planters and sold goods to retailers as well as individual customers. Most commission merchants specialized in an area of trade. In the case of Muscat & Lott, produce was its specialty and it delivered its products by way of mule-drawn carts. As Wilson's photograph shows, Muscat & Lott proclaimed itself the largest produce commission merchant in the South.

The rival to Hammel's store was Gayfer's, located at the southwest corner of Conception and Dauphin Streets. Founded in 1879 by English native Charles John Gayfer (who immigrated by way of Canada) it offered a variety of fine goods for Mobile families. At the time of Wilson's *c*. 1900 photograph, the store operated on the first floor and the Fidelia Club inhabited the upstairs.

Few businesses have been as firmly established as unique to Mobile as Smith's Bakery, founded in 1901. (Gordon Smith was listed in the City Directory as a baker in 1900.) This photograph was taken at the bakery he built on Dauphin Street near Hallet Street. Smith and several of his employees show samples of the bakery's delectable products. Today, a restaurant called The Bakery is housed in Smith's former bakery.

R.O. Harris Store offered bananas and fresh fruits at the corner of Royal and Dauphin Streets, c. 1900. Wilson captured this scene during what appears to be a special occasion—perhaps the Fourth of July—when the storefront is draped with ribbons and American flags.

The fashion for men at the turn of the 20th century was clean-shaven. African-American barbers, above, provided grooming services for white clients. Below are two views of different shops in town. The left photo was taken at Mr. Rose's Barber Shop.

The Bienville Brewery, c. 1901, was a large operation. The line of buildings, from the left, consists of the brew house, bottling plant, and office.

This secluded restaurant offered a quiet spot for dining on Bay Shell Road.

Haas Brother's Southern Market extended itself to customers by making deliveries such as the one here, by delivery wagon, to Happy Hollow Saloon. Even in Wilson's time, businesses were savvy enough marketers to have their company name printed on the delivery vehicle just as is done today.

F.S. Ward Hauling Company delivers a mule-drawn wagon of coal to the Mobile Power Company building.

Employees of Central Trust Bank are, from left to right, Charles Ziegler, unidentified, John McNamara Jr., Bill Strong, Bob McAleer, unidentified, Gonnie Owens, Willie Dwyer, and Lee Ziegler. The Bank of Mobile, National Banking Association Building, left, was located at the corner of St. Michael and Royal Streets. Architect George Rogers had remodeled it.

The stately Cawthon Hotel stood at the southwest corner of St. Francis and Conception Streets, facing Bienville Square. Originally six stories, a seventh floor was added containing a glassed roof garden, which became popular for special events. It was demolished in 1971.

The Boehm Hotel in Springhill was built in 1903 on the southeast corner of Shell Road and McGregor Avenue.

Built in 1852, the grand Battle House Hotel is shown here, ravaged by fire in 1905. The luxurious hotel was designed by New York Architect Frank Andrews and featured a glass-domed lobby and roof garden. The hotel was rebuilt in 1908 but today sits idle, awaiting renovation.

The Bienville Hotel on Bienville Square opened at the corner of St. Joseph and St. Francis Streets in 1900. It offered 85 rooms with cypress paneling, steam heat, and telephones. Each floor was equipped with a parlor for guests to receive visitors. It was later demolished after an unusual conversion into office space.

WATERFRONT

Of most importance to Mobile's economic turn-around was the dredging of the harbor. In 1900, local leaders formed the Mobile Joint Rivers and Harbors Committee, and worked tirelessly for improvements to the waterfront. Federal funds helped support these efforts and, subsequently, river traffic increased. The port diversified as well, with timber, cotton, naval stores, and oysters becoming important exports and fruit a steady import. Cranes, schooners, dredges, barges and steamboats crowded the riverbanks as the port came back to life.

Riverboats *Vienna, Mary*, and others dock at Mobile where numerous bales of cotton await loading.

Seamen pose for Wilson aboard a ship docked at Mobile harbor. A seaworthy dog and cat were included in the portrait. Seafaring crews such as this one were a familiar sight in Mobile at the turn of the century.

The fruit boat *España* unloads at the waterfront dock. By 1904 Mobile was the third-busiest port in the banana trade. Mobile's port was convenient particularly to Central America, a major producer.

A mountain of bananas fills a Mobile warehouse *c.*1900. Exotic fruits were shipped into Mobile from Central America, then resold through local distributors who could sell them locally or ship them north by train.

The schooner *General Whiting* takes on lumber.

Ships dock for loading at Mobile Docks Company's Mobile & Ohio Railroad Warehouse.

The United States Naval vessel *McDonough* drew an interested crowd when it docked at Mobile c. 1900.

Passengers prepare to board the *Pleasure Bay* docked at Mobile.

Schooners, tugboats, and other vessels dock at the busy Mobile waterfront above; a square-rigged schooner, possibly Norwegian, docks at Mobile below.

Tugboats *Resolute* and *Russell* above were typical of vessels involved in waterway commerce c.1900, as was the freighter *Mobila* below.

Wilson chronicled the historic centennial celebration of Fort St. Stephens in 1895. The Spanish built the fort in 1795 at a settlement established by the French. The settlement had also been under English rule. The vessels pictured here are the U.S. Reserve Cutter *Wynona*, which represented the United States government, and the bay boat *James A. Carney*. The *Carney* transported the Spanish Consul and delegation from Mobile to the celebration. The *Wynona*, piloted up the Tombigbee River by Capt. Ed G. Jackson, flew all the flags for such an occasion.

Four

CELEBRATION

MARDI GRAS

In Alabama, Mobile is synonymous with Mardi Gras. The Port City boasts the first American celebration of Mardi Gras, attributable to its French Catholic roots. A French phrase, Mardi Gras translates as "Fat Tuesday," referring to the day before Ash Wednesday and the beginning of Lent when believers began an observation of self-denial and penitence leading to Holy Week and the celebration of Easter, the Church's highest holy day of the year. The reference to fat was connected to the practice of disposing of rich, fatty foods in the household prior to the beginning of Lent through elaborate cooking and feasting.

In modern times Mardi Gras in Mobile has taken on a primarily secular character as it relates to merry-making, dances, and parades. Mobile's sense of celebration in Wilson's day, as now, extended year-round, as is shown in Wilson's photographs of Mardi Gras scenes, as well as special events and organizations that brought citizens together for fellowship.

Robert Neville's automobile was covered with poppies and carried Miss Reba Neville, Miss Saida Billups, Miss Louise Vass, and Miss Eunice Semmes in the 1905 Floral Parade.

King Felix prepares to join the parade in his mule-drawn float.

Semmes auto is all decked out for the floral parade.

Regally gowned and robed, Queen Mary Morris Clarke, daughter of the Honorable Richard Clarke, reigned over Mobile's Mardi Gras in 1905. Her king was Orville Cawthon.

Lucille Ligon (later Mrs. Clinton McCartney) wears an exquisite gown as a member of the Mardi Gras court.

Capturing a brilliant night scene, Wilson shows an illuminated crown on St. Francis Street. This photograph and the two that follow are evidence of what made Wilson a master photographer. Even with today's sophisticated equipment, the night photography Wilson did is difficult to rival.

Government Street, above, and Duncan Place, below, glowed with the warmth and energy of Mardi Gras and the novelty of electric lighting.

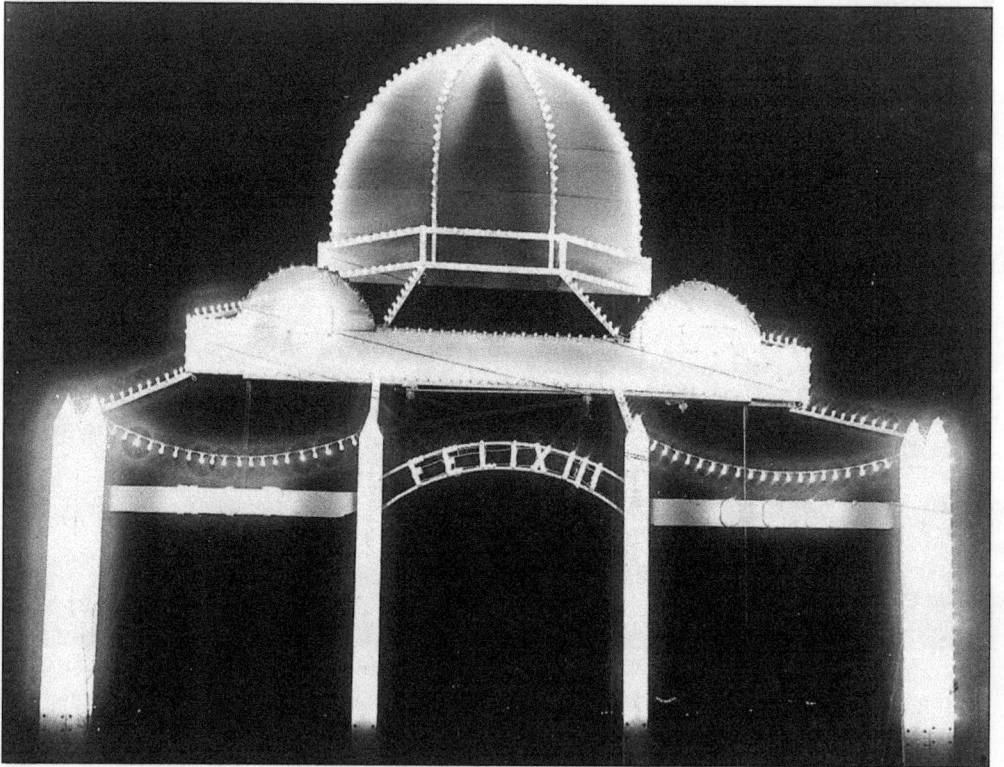

The J.H. Moncrief automobile displays a simple, yet elegant, floral motif in the 1905 Floral Parade.

Yellow mums cover nearly every inch of this automobile, which was also transporting Mrs. Bob Venable, Miss Mastin, Miss M. McKee, and Miss Lizzie Rhett.

John Mahon's automobile was bedecked with a mixture of mums and carried Miss Clara Sims, Miss Claudia Friendenthal, and Miss Marion Mahon.

J.B. Webster's decorated automobile pulled behind it an elaborately decorated cart.

Miss C. Touart, Miss Rose Hayes, and Mrs. T.J. Touart were the passengers in T.J. Touart's automobile in the floral parade.

John van Heuval's automobile was covered with waterlilies and transported these youngsters, from left to right, James van Heuval, John Damrich, Grace van Hueval, Marie Unruh, Irma Unruh, Mabel Hartwell, Allie Yeend, and Gabriella Cooke.

The Richards entry in the 1905 Floral Parade added a colorful if oversized butterfly to its decorations. In front are Mr. and Mrs. Richards. In the rear are Miss May Prince (later Mrs. William Hunter) and Miss Venetia Danner (later Mrs. Clarendon McClure).

After the Civil War, Mobile's annual Mardi Gras was reinstated through the efforts of Joseph Cain and a few of his friends, who staged a spontaneous parade to the wonder of occupying Yankee troops. Cain's creation, Chief Slackabamirimico, has since been immortalized on Joe Cain Day—the Sunday before Fat Tuesday—by many revelers such as these (above). The "Old Chief" himself would probably smile at the Joe Cain follower of 1905 (right).

A Mardi Gras Ball in the ballroom of the Battle House was a grand event in Mobile. The rooftop ballroom featured balconies where bands played for the dancers below. The trellised roof had a wonderful garden.

SPECIAL EVENTS

Events that bring people together are cause for celebration in any city. Mobilians have gathered for civic, social, and family events since the city's founding some 300 years ago.

Monroe Park with its baseball field, picnic area and lake, offered a suitable location for outings south of town. Formal and informal gatherings—dances, parades, picnics, and parties—were all part of the Mobile social scene then as now. Wilson was aware of the significance of such events and recorded them as part of his documentation of life in the Port City at the turn of the twentieth century.

Then former President Theodore Roosevelt was among the luminaries who made visits to Mobile around 1900. Here, he participated in the 1902 dedication of the Masonic building cornerstone.

John Fowler's flying machine was first exhibited in Bienville Square in 1893 and later in Monroe Park, where Wilson photographed it. Operated by spring power, the model was similar to modern machines in its design. Despite impressive demonstrations by Fowler at these public events, he was unable to rouse interest among serious investors and did not get his machine off the ground in time to beat the Wright Brothers to national acclaim.

Ferdinand Karl Jr. and his younger brother celebrated Christmas at home in Mobile in 1904. Riding toys, dolls, and even wooden Indians were among the playthings of almost a century ago that children today would enjoy.

A Christmas tree in the classroom dominated this scene from Barton Academy, reminding students of the message framed and hanging on the wall: "You can if you will."

Just as parents today love to capture the highlights of their children's lives, so did the parents of Wilson's day. This photograph shows a happy "crowd scene" with youngsters gathered to celebrate some lucky child's big day. (Note that the cake in center rear appears to have five lit candles.) The smartly dressed party guests complement the beautifully decorated table, draped with festive ribbons.

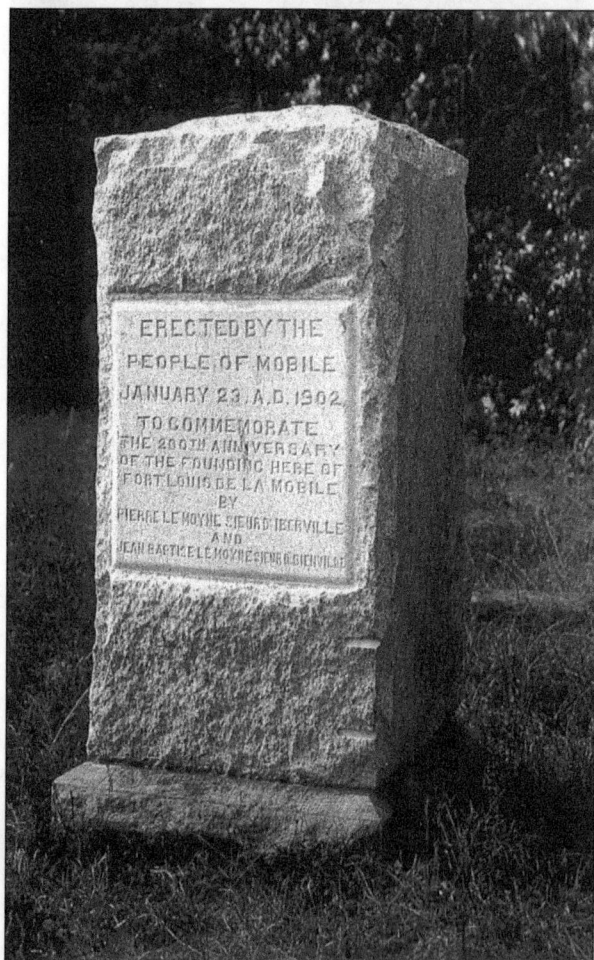

Mobile's bicentennial was a big celebration on January 23, 1902, when a sizeable crowd gathered at the former site of Fort Louis de La Mobile at 27-Mile Bluff. Pierre LeMoyne Sieur d'Iberville and his younger brother, Jean Baptiste Le Moyne Sieur d'Bienville, founded the fort settlement. A marker, left, was placed at the site in conjunction with the celebration.

Baseball had become the Great American Pastime by 1900 and players and fans in Mobile were not immune to its appeal. Here, the Stonewall team prepares to do battle on the baseball diamond at Monroe Park.

Wilson captured the action of baseball with an eye that makes today's sports photographers great. Above, a runner leaves third with scoring on his mind. Below, something of a photo finish was not enough to spare this runner from being tagged out while attempting to slide into base.

ORGANIZATIONS

Social, civic, and professional organizations existed in Wilson's day, much as they do today. However, at the turn of the twentieth century, such organizations would not include members from more than one race or have both male and female members. These guidelines were typical of the Victorian era and did not hamper members from enjoying themselves nor prevent various organizations from contributing to the improvement of life in the city.

There were ethnic considerations among the white community as well. The Althestan Club existed for the Anglo-Saxon political, business, and social elite while the Fidelia Society was established for Jewish men. Along with these were, of course, several mystic societies, fraternal organizations, veterans' groups, militia companies and fire companies, among others.

Members of the Federation of Labor and their guests gathered for a bay boat cruise on the A.S.A. Carney on Mobile Bay.

Members of the Ladies Auxiliary of the Central Trade Council (above and below) were photographed by Wilson, most likely on the occasion of a general meeting or banquet.

Members of the fraternal organization Woodmen of the World (WOW) assemble for a photograph at the bandstand in Bienville Square. Woodmen of the World was started in Omaha, Nebraska, in 1890 and the Mobile chapter was formed shortly after. The national organization exists today, still as a non-profit group that fosters fraternalism, civic commitment, and patriotism. In the early part of the twentieth century, members of WOW were distinguished by their organizational response to communities struck by natural disasters.

Members of Mobile's chapter of the Salvation Army assemble for a photograph by Wilson in the late 1800s. The Salvation Army was founded in London, England, in 1865 and began official work in the United States in 1880. The mission of the Salvation Army—which is an organized church—is to minister to the financially "down and out" in society.

Knights of Columbus Hall on St. Joseph Street served a large fraternal organization of Catholic men in Mobile from the early 1880s. The organization for Catholic men was founded in New Haven, Connecticut, in 1882. The Knights of Columbus, which has several chapters in Mobile today, and has grown to an international organization, has as its goals the strengthening of charity, unity, fraternity, patriotism, and family life.

The Pythian Bethel Cadets were a company of African-American young men trained in the tradition of other military organizations in the city c. 1900.

The Young Men's Christian Association was founded in the United States in 1851 and organized in Mobile in 1856. Mobile's YMCA was going strong in 1904 when Wilson took this photograph inside the building.

Fire protection was a critical need throughout Mobile's early history. In fact, volunteer fire companies in the early nineteenth century were the center of social as well as civic life for many Mobilians. Fire was a constant threat throughout the century and most of the city's original buildings were destroyed by fire. The city's first paid fire department, pictured here, was established in 1888.

Local military companies emerged in Mobile beginning in the late 1830s in response to threats by Creek Indians to violate a treaty. Later, the Mobile Cadets—essentially a group of boys—organized in anticipation of joining American troops in the Mexican War in 1845. It turned out that only a couple of members of the unit met age requirements to serve. Later, when the Civil War started, these local companies saw actual battle. City militia companies were later organized into the Alabama State Militia in 1875. Before and after the conflict, however, the companies often drew crowds of appreciative spectators who watched them parade and drill. Drill competitions such as one held in Mobile on July 4, 1905, featured the Mobile Cadets Company (above) and units such as the two on the next page. The event was held at Monroe Park.

The Lomax Rifles are seen here on July 4, 1905 in Monroe Park.

The Gulf City Guards are seen here on July 4, 1905 in Monroe Park.

Alabama First Regiment encampment is seen above c. 1900. This Mobile encampment was an annual summer event from the late 1800s into the early 20th century.

Troops assemble at encampment.

This photograph shows a review of troops at encampment.

ACKNOWLEDGMENTS

This book has been a labor of love made possible through the assistance and support of several people. Thanks first to my wonderful and talented husband, Art Culpepper, whose technical expertise was essential to the scanning of this collection and whose love and encouragement made the effort manageable. Thanks also to my children, Jared and Miranda, whose willingness to allow me space to do most of this work at home, made the process easier.

Special thanks go to the Mitchell Foundation, which has provided funds throughout the years to secure the preservation of the Wilson collection, most recently through a grant awarded in 2000, which was essential to the completion of this project.

Finally, I wish to thank the people who have in some way assisted with the creation of this book and they are as follows: Jean Wentworth, executive assistant, Historic Mobile Preservation Society; Tom McGehee, author and curator, Bellingrath Home, who wrote some of the introductions (noted at the end of each entry); Herbert Marston, City of Mobile Cemeteries Operations Department; the Very Rev. Michael L. Farmer, chancellor of the Catholic Archdiocese of Mobile; Helen Wilson, historian and editor, *Landmark Letter*; Marylon Barkan, HMPS archives chairman; Patsy Starkey, director, Mobile Medical Museum, for research assistance; John Sledge, historian, Mobile Historic Development Commission; the Executive Board of Historic Mobile Preservation Society for support of this project; and Katie White, Acquisitions Editor, Arcadia Publishing, for her kindness and assistance.

PRIMARY SOURCES

A History of Medicine in Alabama, by Howard L. Holley; *Alabama: The History of a Deep South State*, published by the University of Alabama Press; *Cotton City*, by Harriet Amos; *Craighead's Mobile*, by Caldwell Delaney; *Mobile: American River City*, by Michael Thomason and Melton McLaurin; *Mobile! City by the Bay*, by Jay Higginbotham; *Highlights of 100 Years in Mobile*, published by The First National Bank of Mobile; various articles, *Landmark Letter*, published by Historic Mobile Preservation Society; *Mobile: The Life and Times of a Great Southern City*, by Melton McLaurin and Michael Thomason; articles from *The Harbinger* series, "Mobile Then & Now," by Tom McGehee; *The Story of Mobile*, Caldwell Delaney; *Victorian and Edwardian Fashion*, Alison Gernsheim.